duck

apple

My First
1000
Words & Pictures

tractor

egg

Brown Watson

ENGLAND

Contents

ISBN 978-0-7097-1878-9
First published 2010 by Brown Watson
The Old Mill, 76 Fleckney Road,
Kibworth Beauchamp,
LE8 0HG, ENGLAND

The Family

father, dad

mother, mum

grandfather (father's father)

grandmother, (father's mother)

son, brother

daughter, sister

cousin (uncle's son)

cousin (aunt's daughter)

aunt (mother's sister)

uncle (mother's brother)

Our Bodies

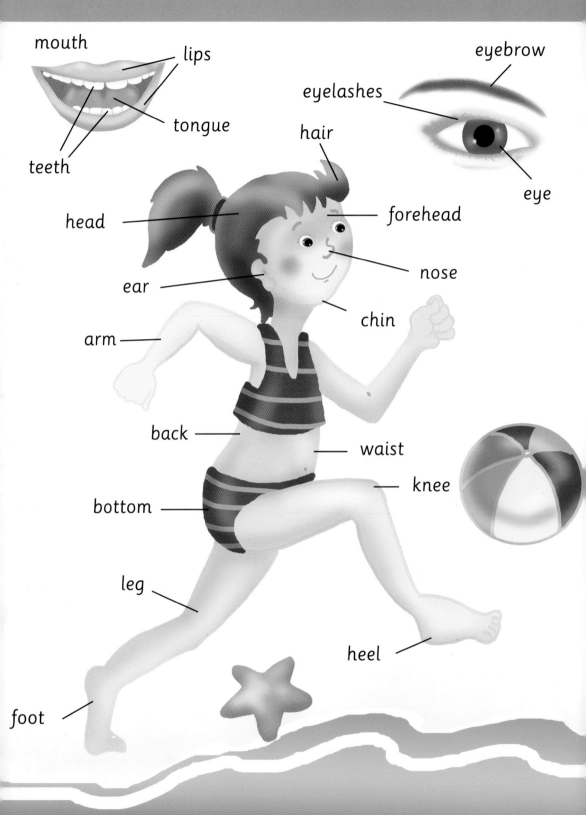

mouth

lips

tongue

teeth

eyelashes

eyebrow

eye

hair

head

forehead

nose

ear

chin

arm

back

waist

knee

bottom

leg

heel

foot

Our Bodies

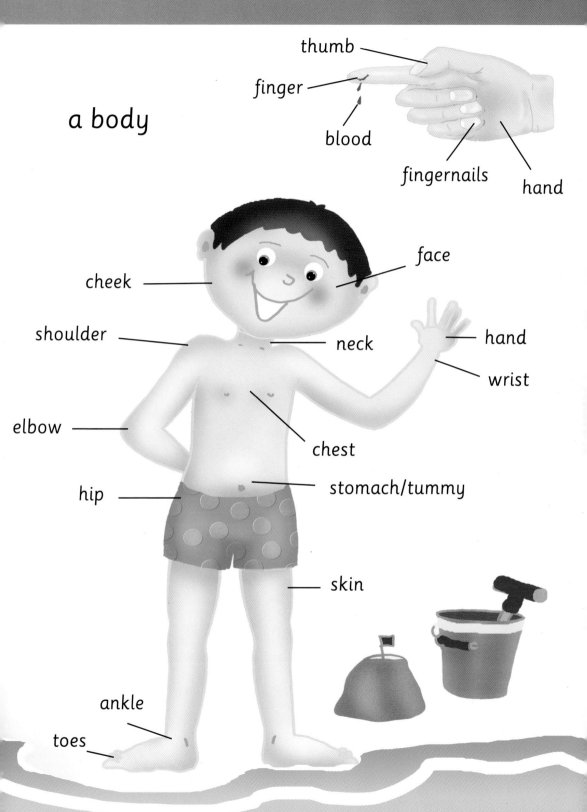

a body

thumb

finger

blood

fingernails

hand

cheek

face

shoulder

neck

hand

wrist

elbow

chest

hip

stomach/tummy

skin

ankle

toes

More People Words

family

parents

twins

man

child

boy

girl

teenager

woman

More People Words

wife

husband

friends

step-sister

step-brother

triplets

baby

Clothes

dress

sweater

hat

coat

knickers

dressing gown

trousers

anorak

socks

blouse

cap

leggings

skirt

pyjamas

sun dress

Clothes

shorts

raincoat

T-shirt

ties

dungarees

underslip

trousers

nightie

waistcoat

rain hat

cardigan

shirt

tracksuit

jumper

More Things to Wear

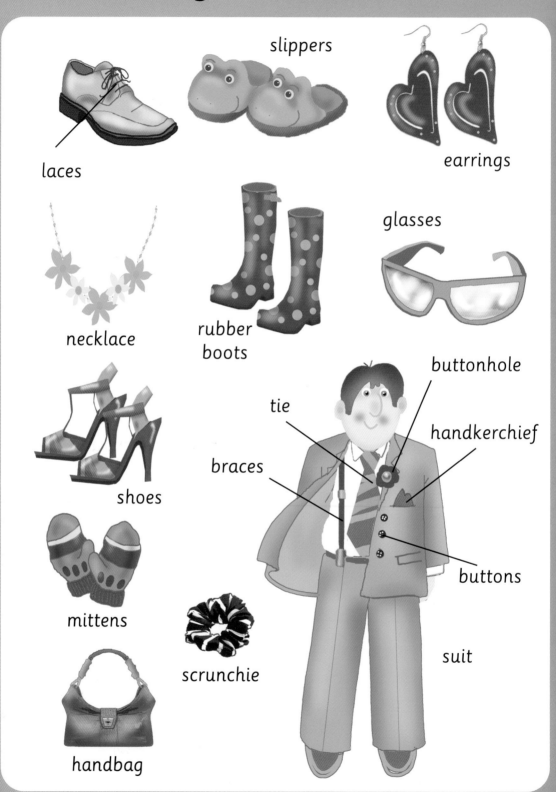

slippers

laces

earrings

necklace

rubber boots

glasses

shoes

buttonhole

tie

handkerchief

braces

buttons

mittens

scrunchie

suit

handbag

More Things to Wear

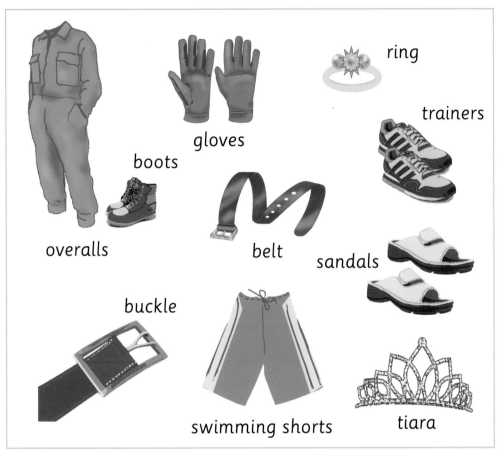

ring

trainers

gloves

boots

overalls

belt

sandals

buckle

swimming shorts

tiara

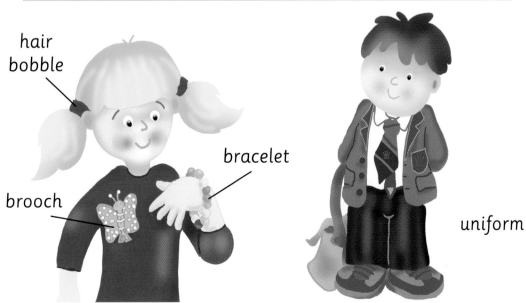

hair
bobble

bracelet

brooch

uniform

The Bedroom

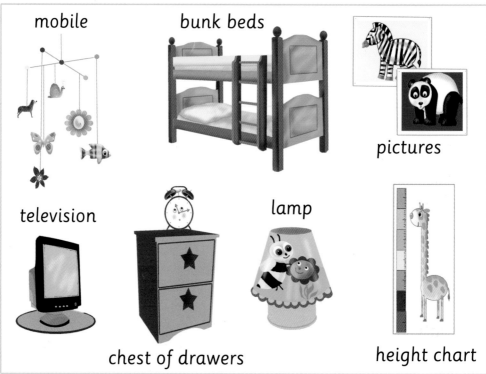

mobile

bunk beds

pictures

television

chest of drawers

lamp

height chart

The Bedroom

window

curtains

alarm clock

cot

rug

bed

cushion

duvet

pillow

wardrobe

cradle

The Bathroom

plug

plughole

sponge

bath

bubbles

toilet

toilet paper

The Bathroom

towel

wash basin

shower curtain

taps

soap dish

towel rail

soap

toothpaste

shower

toothbrush

potty

scales

The Kitchen

food mixer

microwave

kettle

oven

cupboard

sink

draining board

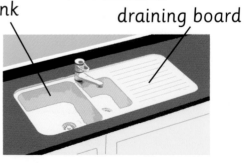

teapot

vacuum cleaner

mugs

iron

ironing board

washing machine

dishwasher

switches

socket

freezer

electric plug

refrigerator/fridge

The Living Room

picture frame

door

handle

magazine rack

magazines

cushions

newspapers

The Living Room

painting

telephone

remote control

mobile phone

television set/TV

mp3 player

radiator

mantelpiece

dvd player

fireplace

vase of flowers

The Dining Room

tablecloth

plates

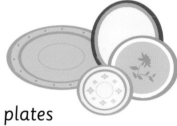

cup

vinegar

oil

saucer

teaspoon

mirror

The Dining Room

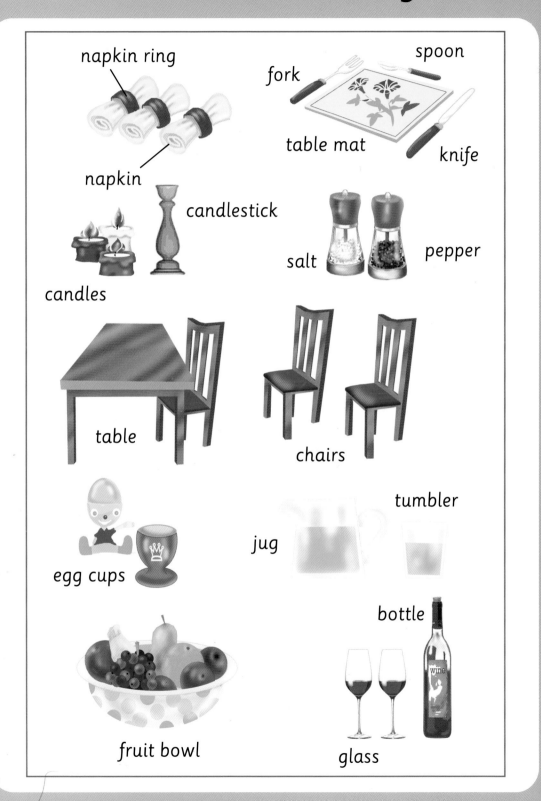

napkin ring

spoon

fork

table mat

knife

napkin

candlestick

salt

pepper

candles

table

chairs

tumbler

jug

egg cups

bottle

fruit bowl

glass

The Playroom

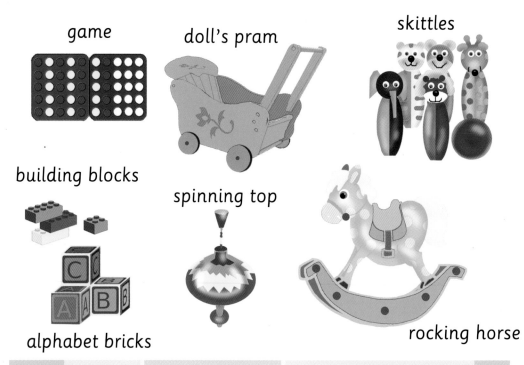

game

doll's pram

skittles

building blocks

spinning top

alphabet bricks

rocking horse

toys

The Playroom

doll's house

robot

toy dinosaur

computer game

soft toys

toy cars

skateboard

toy boats

toy soldiers

train station

castle

train

Things in the House

footstool

settee

rocking chair

beanbag

stool

high chair

rug

laptop computer

Things in the House

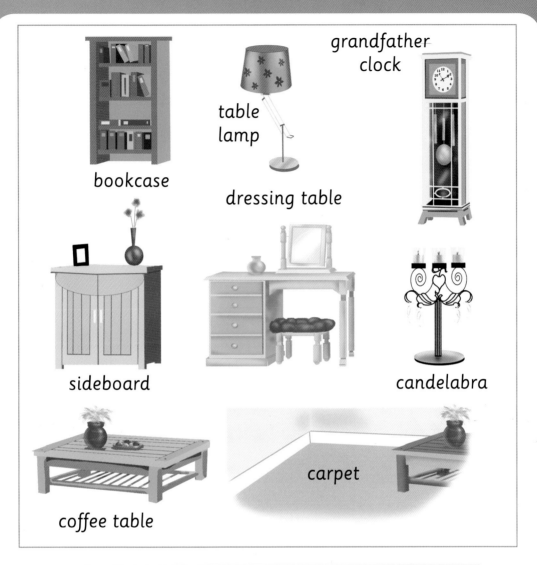

bookcase

table lamp

grandfather clock

dressing table

sideboard

candelabra

coffee table

carpet

breakfast bar

The Garden

The Garden

pond

greenhouse

window box

garden tools

shed

bird table

barbeque

wheelbarrow

lawnmower

umbrella

table

chairs

seeds

rake

fork

sprinkler

plant pot

carrots

spade

lettuce

hosepipe

The House

window

satellite dish

front door

door knocker

garage

chimney

roof

doormat

driveway

refuse bin

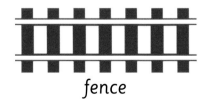
fence

wall

In the Workshop

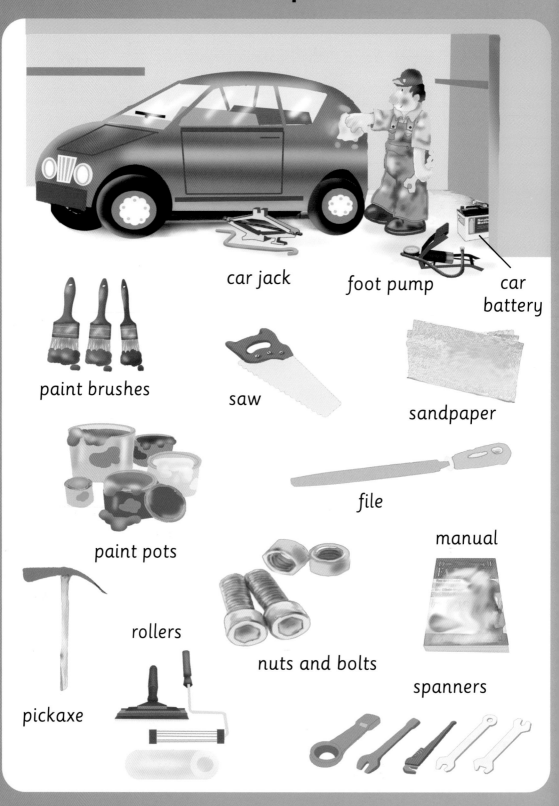

car jack

foot pump

car battery

paint brushes

saw

sandpaper

paint pots

file

manual

rollers

nuts and bolts

spanners

pickaxe

In the Workshop

oilcan

vice

axe

wooden plank

drill

penknife

screwdriver

screws

pliers

nails

bucket

hammer

toolbox

tape measure

plane

Friendly Pets

mouse

goldfinch

toad

guinea pig

parrot

kitten

cat

hamster

budgerigar

canary

cockerel

rat

donkey

horse

foal

Friendly Pets

duck

hedgehog

mynah bird

fish tank

tropical
fish

dog

rabbit

puppy

cockatoo

lizard

gerbil

Out in the Street

bus stop

traffic lights

parking meter

traffic cone

lamppost

road works

road sign

level crossing

Out in the Street

lorry

bus

truck

digger

bicycle

motorcycle

taxi

police car

car

fire engine

In the Town

church

restaurant

factory

cinema

theatre

hotel

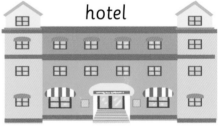

park

office block

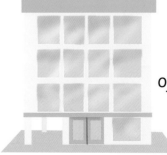

In the Town

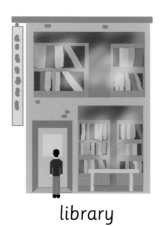

library

bank

skyscraper

sports stadium

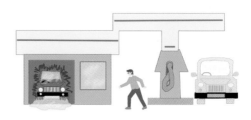

garage

supermarket

florist

houses

bar

In the Supermarket

checkout

In the Supermarket

trolley

bread

vegetables

strawberries

milk

soup

basket

fish

peppers

mushrooms

cheese

money

credit card

purse

chip and
pin machine

breakfast
cereal

carrier bag

chiller cabinet

turkey

toilet rolls

Fruit

grapes

banana

orange

lemon

cherries

pineapple

apple

redcurrants

plums

gooseberries

grapefruit

pear

melon

strawberries

blackberries

Vegetables

green beans

tomatoes

cucumber

potatoes

cabbage

peas

corn on the cob

leeks

onions

carrots

cauliflower

mushrooms

lettuce

pumpkin

brussels sprouts

More things to Eat and Drink

can of soup

buns

nuts

honey

sandwich

ice cream

sweets

pizza

spaghetti

eggs

lollipops

toast

doughnuts

coconut

chocolate bar

milk

burger

crisps

bottle of cola

More things to Eat and Drink

cakes

fish fingers

jelly

hot dog

fries

tomato sauce

milk shakes

sausage roll

apple pie

salad

loaf of bread

pancakes

rice

Fun in the Park

Fun in the Park

climbing frame

roundabout

kite

helmet

litter bin

park bench

pads

bandstand

skateboard

scooter

sandpit

fountain

toy yacht

slide

dog

pond

notice board

ball

seesaw

People at Work

electrician

hairdresser

shop keeper

ringmaster

scientist

librarian

fashion designer

dentist

traffic warden

People at Work

security guard

miner

baker

judge

dancer

refuse collector

singer

doctor

policeman

More People at Work

artist

gardener

waiter

clown

window cleaner

fireman

carpenter

musician

actor

decorator

cameraman

teacher

secretary

ABCDEFGHI
JKLMNOPQR
STUVWXYZ
12345678910

More People at Work

farmer

fisherman

postman

diver

chef

mechanic

removal man

nurse

butcher

vet

photographer

builder

astronaut

In the Office

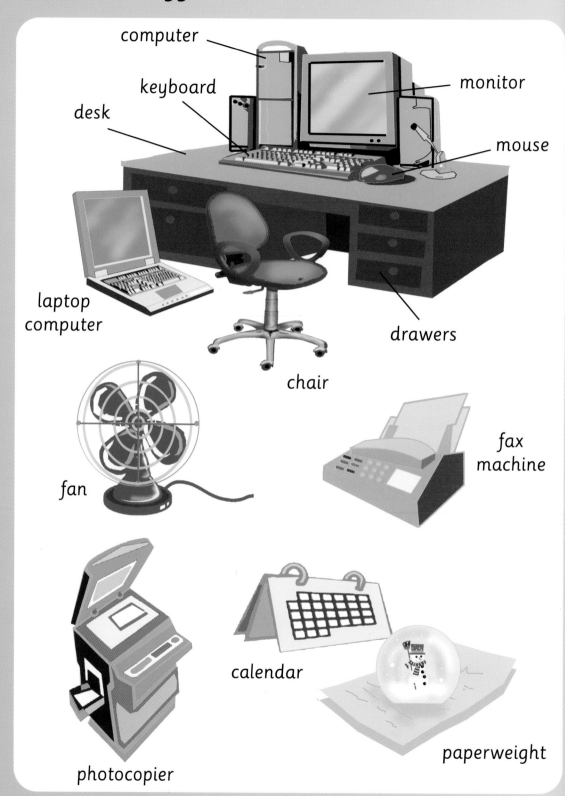

computer

keyboard

desk

monitor

mouse

laptop computer

drawers

chair

fan

fax machine

photocopier

calendar

paperweight

In the Office

filing cabinet

calculator

pencil

pen

rubber

ruler

pencil sharpener

coffee machine

stapler

wastepaper bin

envelopes

paper

At the Garage

car wash

cashier

puddle of oil

breakdown vehicle

petrol tanker

PETROL

petrol pumps

attendant

water pump

air pump

At the Garage

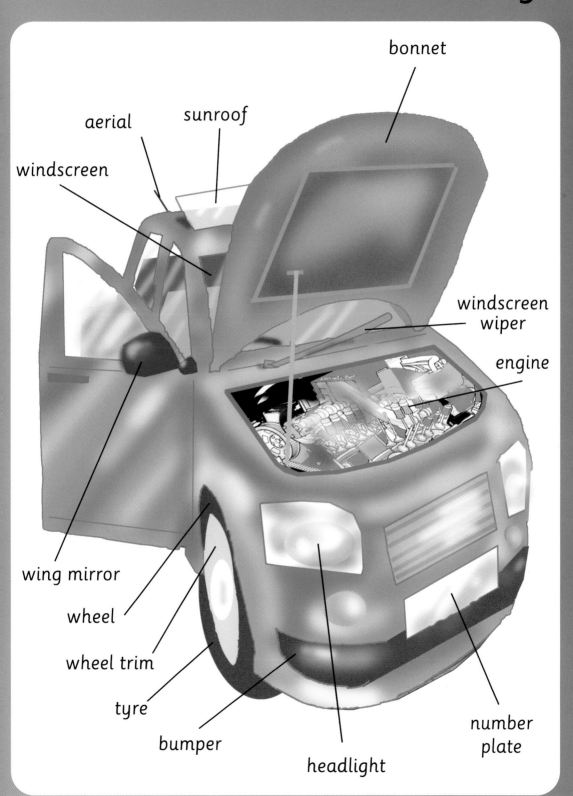

bonnet

aerial

sunroof

windscreen

windscreen wiper

engine

wing mirror

wheel

wheel trim

tyre

bumper

headlight

number plate

At the Doctor

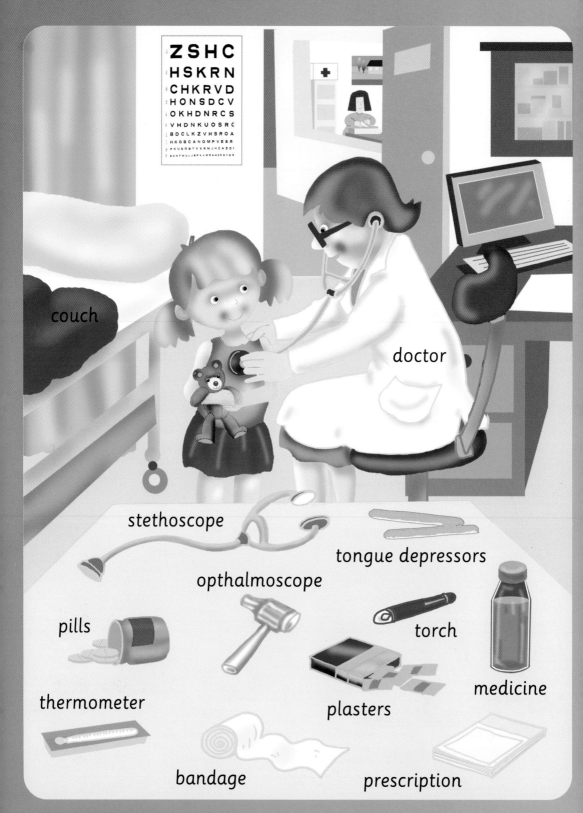

couch

doctor

stethoscope

tongue depressors

opthalmoscope

torch

pills

medicine

thermometer

plasters

bandage

prescription

At the Dentist

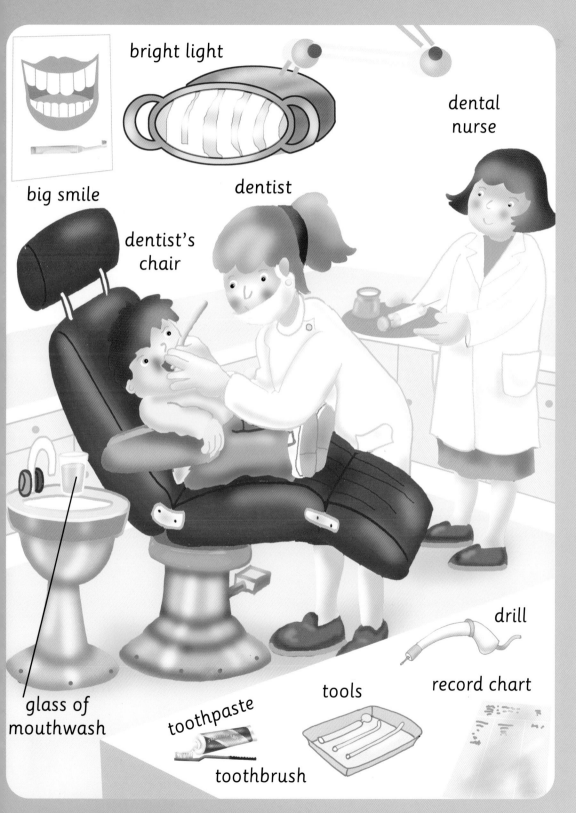

bright light

dental nurse

big smile

dentist

dentist's chair

glass of mouthwash

toothpaste

toothbrush

tools

drill

record chart

In Hospital

In Hospital

crutches

medication

x-ray

thermometer

bandage

get well card

tray

plaster

wheelchair

syringe

water bottle

clipboard

vase of flowers

bowl of fruit

Games and Pastimes

cutting
and sticking

dancing

listening to music

gardening

sewing

playing a board game

reading

Games and Pastimes

cooking

writing

walking

leapfrog

singing

playing a
computer game

playing cards

dressing up

Sports

horse riding

cycling

ice hockey

basketball

golf

skiing

swimming

boxing

ice skating

baseball

Sports

rugby

cricket

football

gymnastics

tennis

badminton

running

On the Farm

apple trees

farmer

dog

haystack

tractor

horse

foal

goose

goslings

turkey

cockerel

duck

ducklings

On the Farm

cow

hen

chicks

calf

pig

sheep

lamb

piglet

goat

kid

bull

At School

lunch box

globe

computer

modelling
clay

notebook

**ABCDEFGHI
JKLMNOPQR
STUVWXYZ
1234567891O**

alphabet

At School

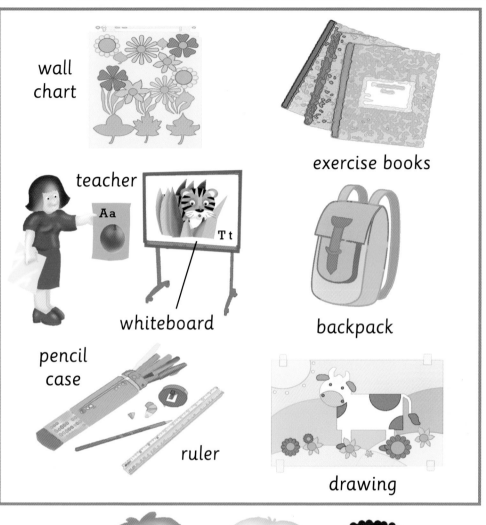

wall chart

exercise books

teacher

Aa

Tt

whiteboard

backpack

pencil case

ruler

drawing

pupils

Going Places: By Train

the railway station

monorail

diesel engine

steam engine

goods wagon

platform

escalator

Going Places: By Train

buffet car/carriage

luggage

ticket office

signal

buffer

passenger

monitor

ticket collector

level crossing

Going Places: By Water

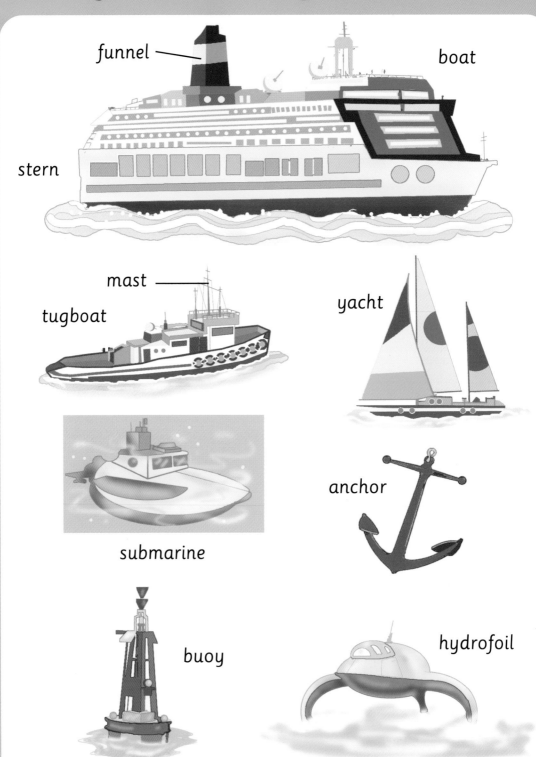

funnel

boat

stern

mast

tugboat

yacht

submarine

anchor

buoy

hydrofoil

Going Places: By Water

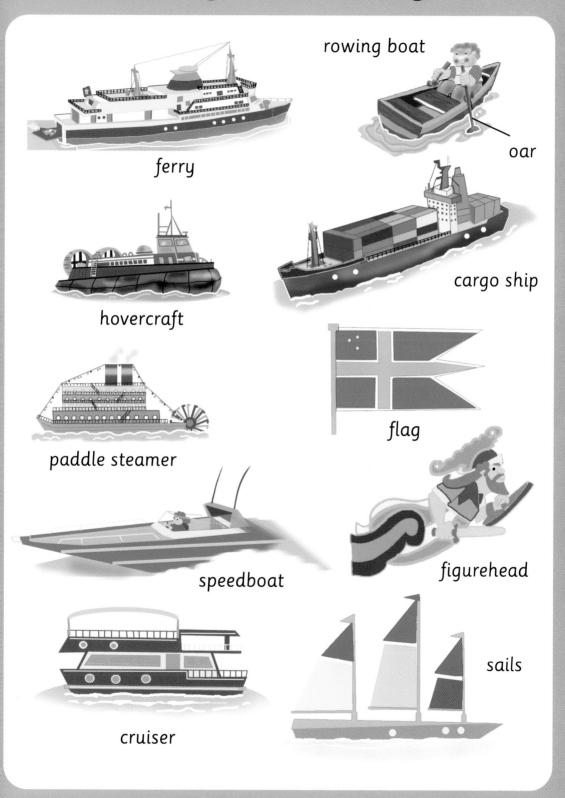

ferry

rowing boat

oar

hovercraft

cargo ship

paddle steamer

flag

speedboat

figurehead

cruiser

sails

Going Places: By Plane

biplane

monoplane

triplane

helicopter

fuel tanker

Going Places: By Plane

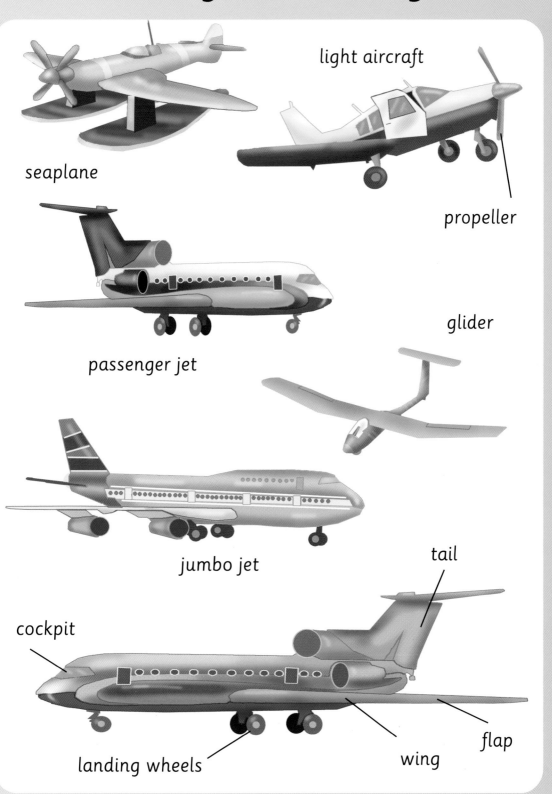

light aircraft

seaplane

propeller

passenger jet

glider

jumbo jet

tail

cockpit

flap

landing wheels

wing

In the Country

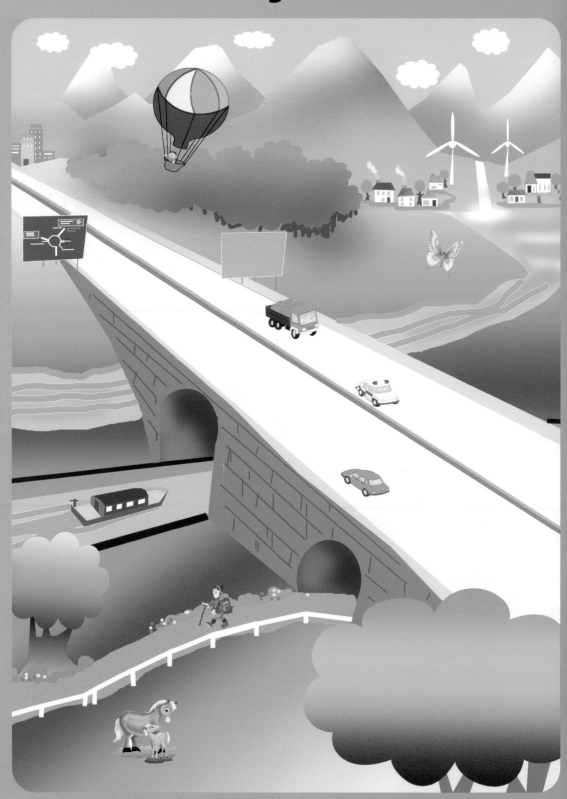

In the Country

wild flowers

caravan

hiker

map

tent

camp fire

scarecrow

trees

butterfly

village

hot air
balloon

hedgehog

fisherman

rabbit

mountains

Builders and Buildings

fire station

cottage

mosque

boathouse

castle

hospital

stately home

terraced houses

car park

hangar

Builders and Buildings

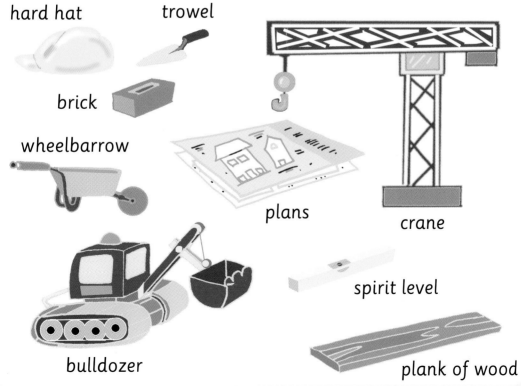

hard hat

trowel

brick

wheelbarrow

plans

crane

spirit level

bulldozer

plank of wood

Seasons and Weather

rainbow

spring

sunshine

storm

lightning   rain

summer

Seasons and Weather

autumn

wind

snow

winter

ice

Wild Animals

tiger

zebra

armadillo

panda

elephant

crocodile

rhinoceros /rhino

hippopotamus /hippo

lion

monkey

porcupine

Wild Animals

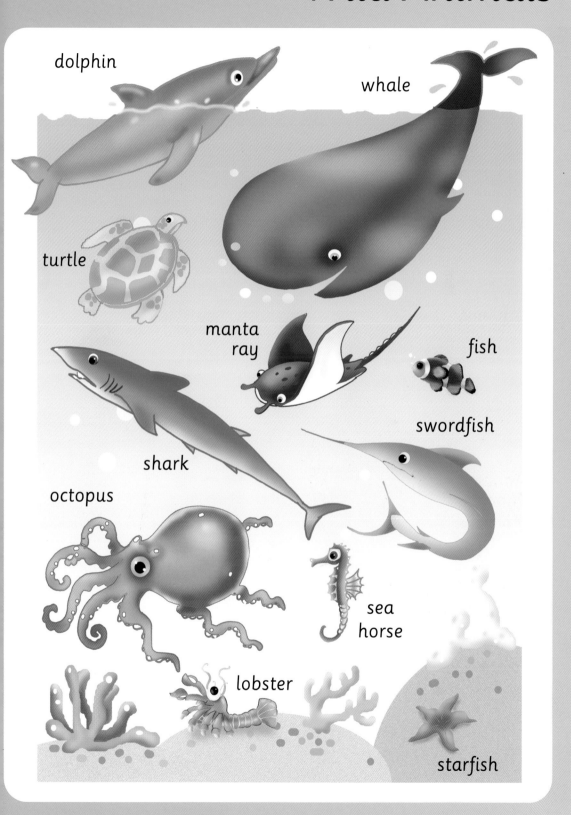

dolphin

whale

turtle

manta ray

fish

swordfish

shark

octopus

sea horse

lobster

starfish

More Wild Animals

penguin

walrus

seal

polar bear

moose

koala

kangaroo

swan

woodpecker

owl

platypus

More Wild Animals

sloth

leopard

gorilla

giraffe

ostrich

boa
constrictor

stork

cobra

peacock

camel

Insects and Creepy-Crawlies

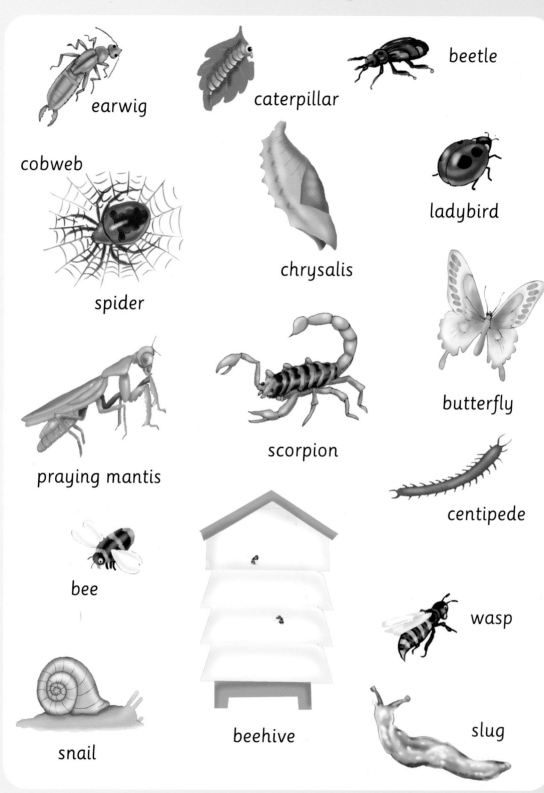

earwig

caterpillar

beetle

cobweb

ladybird

chrysalis

spider

butterfly

praying mantis

scorpion

centipede

bee

wasp

snail

beehive

slug

Animal Parts

wing

beak

antlers

hoof

fin

pouch

flipper

feather

hump

tusk

trunk

whiskers

shell

tail

paw

Plants

shoots

bush

bramble

indoor plant

petal

bud

stem

leaf

bulb

seeds

roots

holly

rushes

twig

cactus

branch

trunk

Flowers

tulip

rose

wild flowers

poppy

gerbera

bouquet

bluebell

sunflower

daffodil

marigold

orchid

Beside the Sea

donkey

umbrella

crab

fishing boat

sunglasses

Beside the Sea

ice cream

seagull

lighthouse

shell

jellyfish

sandcastles

bucket

ball

deckchair

snorkel

spade

seaweed

flip flops

flippers

life buoy

starfish

fishing net

beach mat

Having a Party

Having a Party

paper hat

ice cream

pizza

sweets

present

balloon

crisps

birthday cake

candle

birthday card

fizzy drink

sandwiches

biscuits

jug of orange

fairy cakes

straw

camera

Opposites

fast

slow

up

down

above

below

high

wet

dry

Opposites

over

behind

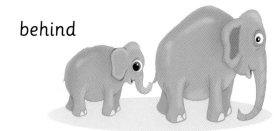

in front

under

big

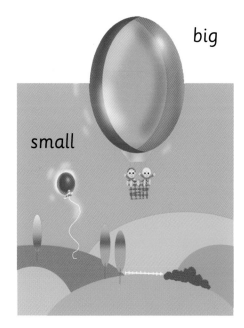

small

thin

fat

out

in

happy

sad

Actions

sitting

walking

reading

drinking

crying

kicking

shouting

playing

cutting

eating

climbing

Actions

writing

drawing

jumping

laughing

blowing

running

cuddling

reaching

knocking

hiding

clapping

pointing

Storybook Words

ghost

monster

mermaid

dinosaur

witch

broomstick

fairy

frog

pirate

Frankenstein's monster

Storybook Words

pixie

wizard

prince

dragon

fire

giant

wolf

princess

knight

Colours and Shapes

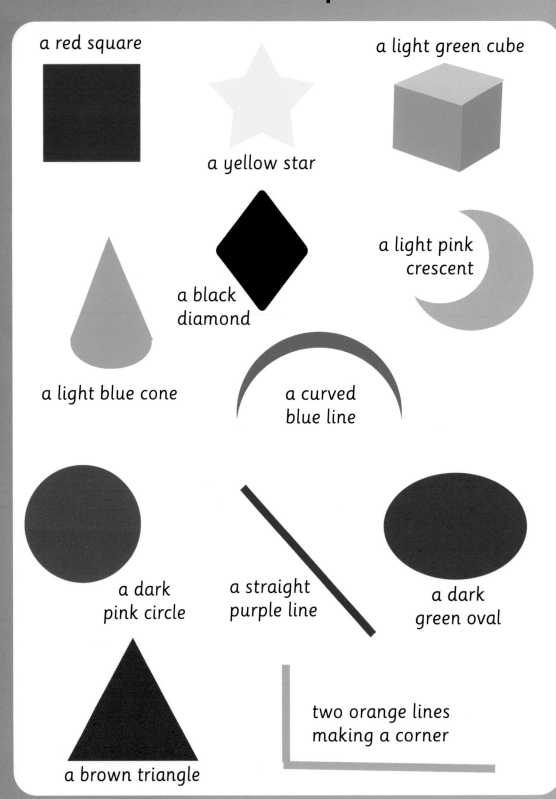

a red square

a yellow star

a light green cube

a black diamond

a light pink crescent

a light blue cone

a curved blue line

a dark pink circle

a straight purple line

a dark green oval

a brown triangle

two orange lines making a corner

Numbers

one

two

three

four

five

six

seven

eight

nine

ten

Days and Months

days of the week

monday

tuesday

wednesday

thursday

friday

saturday

sunday

months of the year

january

february

march

april

may

june

july

august

september

october

november

december

98

Special Days

birthday

holiday

wedding day

Christmas day

The Fairground

shooting gallery

candy floss

popcorn

strength hammer

big wheel

ghost train

hoopla

The Fairground

roller coaster

carousel

dodgems

helter skelter

The Circus

The Circus

circus tent

lion

ball

clown

hoop

acrobat

juggling batons

trapeze artist

dog

elephant

unicyclist

ringmaster

bareback rider

The Restaurant

restaurant

food

dessert

cutlery

tray

The Restaurant

table and chairs

menu

chef

head waiter

waiter

waitress

The Cinema

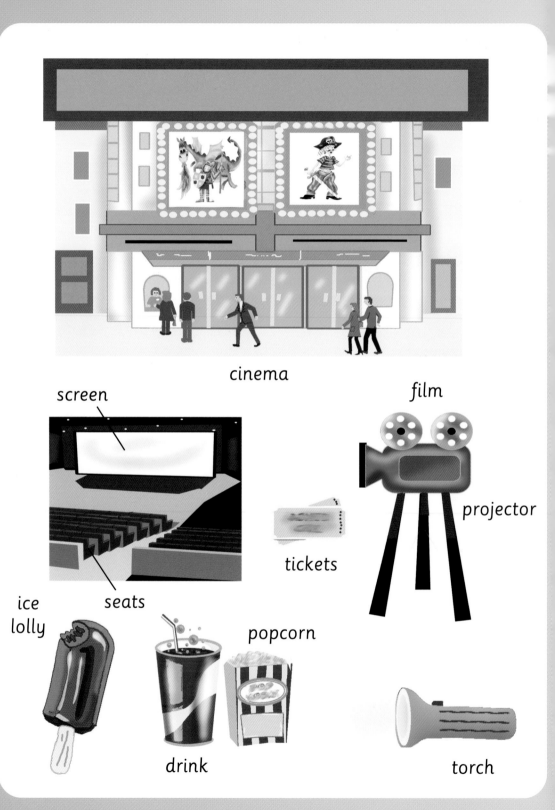

cinema

screen

seats

ice lolly

film

projector

tickets

popcorn

drink

torch

Fun with Colour

paintbrush

crayon

colouring pencil

tube of paint

paper

Fancy Dress

cowboy

pirate

american indian

cow

bunny

fairy

princess

witch

skeleton

Musical Instruments

drum

saxophone

tambourine

violin

recorder

accordion

trumpet

maracas

harp

triangle

horn

cello

bagpipes

xylophone

flute

piano

Baby Things

booties

bib

rattle

bottle

nappy

romper suit

teddy

baby

dummy

bag

blanket

Baby Things

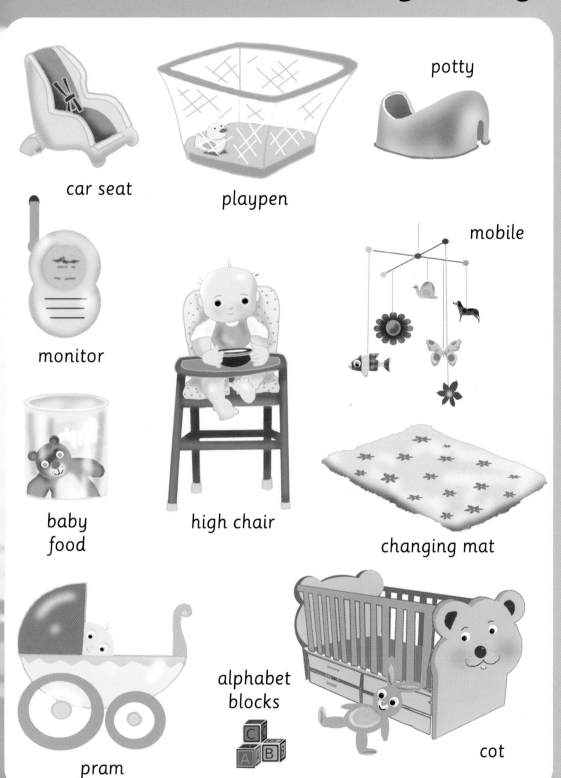

car seat

playpen

potty

monitor

mobile

baby
food

high chair

changing mat

pram

alphabet
blocks

cot

Senses

see

taste

smell

hear

touch

Our Bodies

brain

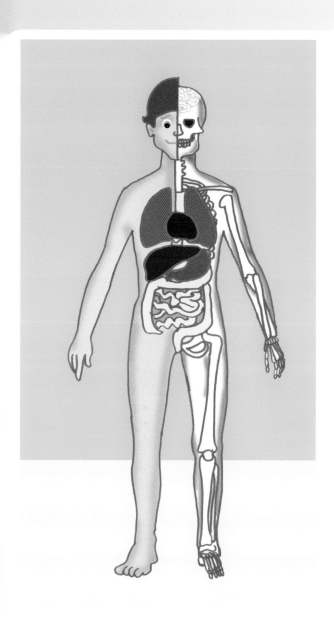

lungs

heart

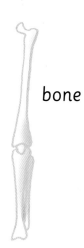
bone

muscle

Space

Space

moon

space shuttle

satellite

planet

meteor

shooting star

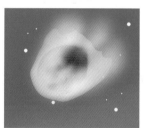

earth

sun

stars

astronaut

Continents of the World

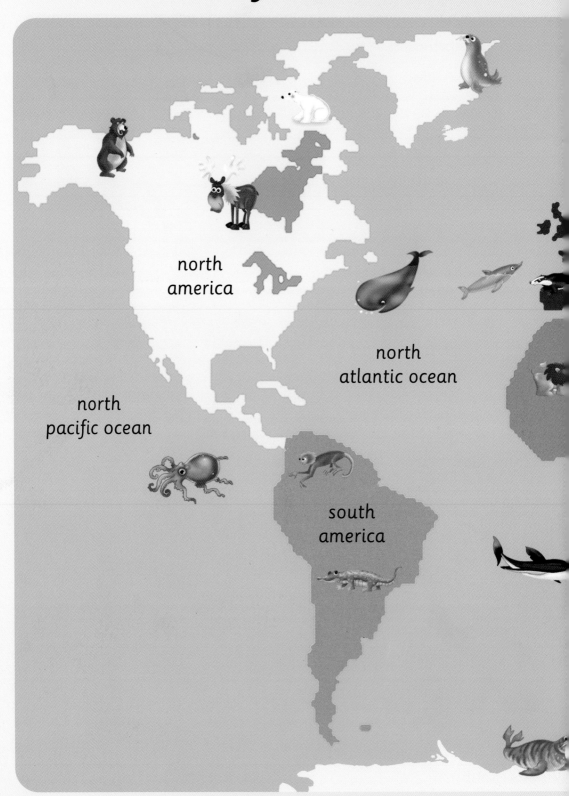

north
america

north
atlantic ocean

north
pacific ocean

south
america

Continents of the World

arctic ocean

asia

europe

africa

north pacific ocean

indian ocean

australia

south atlantic ocean

south pacific ocean

antarctica

Time of Day

morning

daytime

lunchtime

afternoon

evening

night-time

Words in this Book

Words in this Book

Words in this Book

Words in this Book

Words in this Book

Words in this Book

Words in this Book

Words in this Book

Words in this Book

Words in this Book

traffic warden 46
train 23, 66-67
train station 23
trainers 11
trapeze artist 103
tray 57, 104
trees 62, 73
triangle 96, 109
triplane 70
triplets 7
trolley 39
tropical fish 33
trousers 8, 9
trowel 75
truck 35
trumpet 109
trunk (elephant) 83
trunk (tree) 84
t-shirt 9
tube of paint 107
tuesday 98
tugboat 68
tulip 85
tumbler 21
tummy 5
turkey 39, 62
turtle 79
tusk 83
twig 84
twins 6
two 97
tyre 53

uU
umbrella 27, 86
uncle 3
under 91
underslip 9
unicyclist 103
uniform 11
up 90

vV
vacuum cleaner 17
vase 19, 57
vegetables 39
vet 49
vice 31
village 73
vinegar 20
violin 109

wW
waist 4
waistcoat 9
waiter 48, 105
waitress 105
walking 59, 92
wall 29
wall chart 65
walrus 80
wardrobe 13
wash basin 15
washing machine 17
wasp 82
wastepaper bin 51
water 68-69
water bottle 57
water pump 52
weather 76-77
wedding day 99
wednesday 98
weeks 98
wet 90
whale 79
wheel 53
wheel trim 53
wheelbarrow 27, 75
wheelchair 57
whiskers 83
whiteboard 65
wife 7
wild animals 78-81

wild flowers 73, 85
wind 77
window 13, 29
window box 27
window cleaner 48
windscreen 53
windscreen
wiper 53
wing 71, 83
wing mirror 53
winter 77
witch 94, 108
wizard 95
wolf 95
woman 6
wood 75
wooden plank 31
woodpecker 80
work 46-49
workshop 30-31
world 116-117
wrist 5
writing 59, 93

xX
x-ray 57
xylophone 109

yY
yacht 68
year 98
yellow 96

zZ
zebra 78

128